Kid Pick!

Title: _____

Author: _____

Picked by: _____ 910

_____

Why I love this book:

_____

_____

_____

_____

EARTH'S CONTINENTS

South America

by Mary Lindeen

South America is the fourth-largest **continent** in the world. It is south of North America. The tip of South America almost reaches Antarctica.

Arctic Ocean

NORTH
AMERICA

EUROPE

ASIA

Atlantic
Ocean

AFRICA

Pacific
Ocean

SOUTH
AMERICA

Indian
Ocean

Pacific
Ocean

AUSTRALIA

N

W   E

S

Atlantic
Ocean

ANTARCTICA

South America is one of seven continents on Earth.

South America is between two oceans. The Pacific Ocean is to the west of South America. The Atlantic Ocean is to the east.

Some beaches in South America face the Atlantic Ocean.

South America has tall mountains. It also has flat **grasslands**.

The Andes Mountains are in South America.

The world's largest **rain forest** is in South America. It is called the Amazon rain forest. Many unusual plants and animals live there.

Many rare animals live in the Amazon rain forest.

The Amazon River flows through the Amazon rain forest. The Amazon is the second-longest river in the world.

The Amazon River is 4,000 miles (6,437 km) long.

Many of the people in South America live and work on farms. Crops such as fruit and wheat are grown there. Other farmers raise cattle.

Bananas are an important crop in South America.

There are also big cities in South America. Millions of people live in these cities.

Santiago is the capital of Chile, a **country** in South America.

People visit South America to enjoy **festivals**. They also go to the beaches and the mountains.

Dancers perform during a festival in South America.

South America has **ruins** such as Machu Picchu.* Some ruins are thousands of years old. Many people visit South America to see them.

*Say it! *MAH-choo PEEK-choo*

Machu Picchu is in the country of Peru.

South America is home to many interesting people and places. What would you like to see in South America?

*Say it! *EE-gwah-SOO*

Many people visit South America's Iguaçu* Falls.

Glossary

continent (KON-tuh-nent): A continent is one of seven large land areas on Earth. South America is a continent.

country (KUN-tree): A country is an area of land with its own government. Chile is a country in South America.

festivals (FESS-tuh-vulz): Festivals are celebrations. Many people visit South America to attend festivals.

grasslands (GRASS-lands): Grasslands are large open areas of grass where animals can graze. In South America, cattle graze in the grasslands.

rain forest (RAYN FOR-ist): A rain forest is a hot forest where a lot of rain falls. Millions of kinds of animals and insects live in the rain forest.

ruins (ROO-ins): Ruins are the remains of cities or buildings that were abandoned or destroyed a long time ago. Machu Picchu are ruins in South America.

To Find Out More

Books

Aloian, Molly, and Bobbi Kalman. *Explore South America*. New York: Crabtree Publishing, 2007.

Fowler, Allan. *South America*. Danbury, CT: Children's Press, 2001.

Sayre, April Pulley. *South America, Surprise!* Brookfield, CT: Millbrook Press, 2003.

Web Sites

Visit our Web site for links about South America: *childsworld.com/links*

Note to Parents, Teachers, and Librarians: We routinely verify our Web links to make sure they are safe and active sites. So encourage your readers to check them out!

Index

About the Author

Mary Lindeen is an elementary school teacher who turned her love of children and books into a career in publishing. She has written and edited many library books and literacy programs. She also enjoys traveling with her son, Benjamin, whenever and wherever she can.

On the cover: Two llamas living in Bolivia's Sajama National Park.

Published by The Child's World®
1980 Lookout Drive • Mankato, MN 56003-1705
800-599-READ • www.childsworld.com

ACKNOWLEDGMENTS
The Child's World®: Mary Berendes, Publishing Director
The Design Lab: Design, page, and map production
Red Line Editorial: Editorial direction

PHOTO CREDITS: Danny Warren/iStockphoto, cover; Big Stock
Photo, 5, 11, 17, 21; Steve Estvanik/123rf, 7; Luis Louro/123rf, 9;
Michael Zysman/123rf, 13; Raul Rosa/Big Stock Photo, 15;
Michael Klenetsky/123rf, 19

Printed in the United States of America in Mankato, Minnesota.
November 2009
F11460

LIBRARY OF CONGRESS CATALOGING-IN-PUBLICATION DATA
Lindeen, Mary.
  South America / by Mary Lindeen.
    p. cm. — (Earth's continents)
  Includes index.
  ISBN 978-1-60253-352-3 (library bound : alk. paper)
  1. South America—Juvenile literature. I. Title. II. Series.
  F2208.5.L56 2010
  980—dc22   2009030016